Peak District
VILLAGES

First published in 2006 by
Myriad Books Limited,
35 Bishopsthorpe Road,
London SE26 4PA

Photographs and text
copyright © Simon Kirwan

ISBN 1 904 736 24 6

Artwork and design by
Phillip Appleton

Printed in China

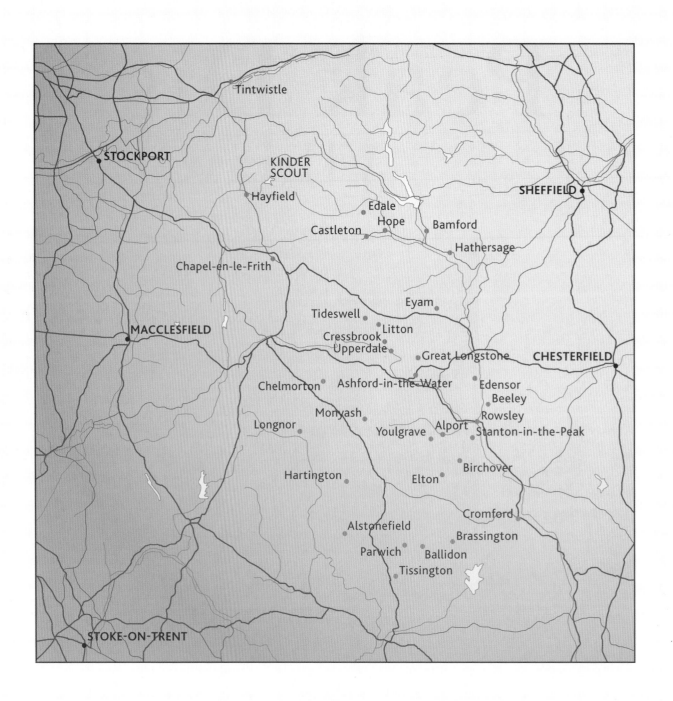

CONTENTS

ALPORT

The picturesque hamlet of Alport is situated three miles south of Bakewell, on the eastern edge of the Peak District National Park

Located at a dreamy spot where the Bradford and Lathkill rivers meet, Alport is a typical limestone village. The river Lathkill descends through the village in a series of cascades, which are pictured here. The Bradford disappeared underground for several years in the 1880s, following the path of an underground drainage canal constructed to prevent water flooding the many leadmines in the surrounding area. Although many of the pretty limestone cottages date back to the 17th and 18th centuries, the village can trace its history back even further to the time of a Saxon settlement.

ALSTONEFIELD

Standing high above sea level on a limestone plateau, Alstonefield is two miles north of Dovedale. It was an important market town until it was overtaken by nearby Ashbourne

Situated on the beautiful river Dove, Alstonefield contains many interesting old buildings, including an ancient tithe barn, situated behind the 16th-century rectory. The church of St Peter has a doorway and chancel arch which dates back to Norman times; the rest of the church was rebuilt and extended several times in the intervening centuries. Next to the village green, the George is a former coaching inn, and behind it is the site of the once-thriving wool market. Alstonefield is the home of the Hope House Costume Museum, which contains a large collection of outfits dating back to the 18th century.

ASHBOURNE

Located at the southern tip of Derbyshire, near the Staffordshire border, Ashbourne is a charming Peak District market town. It is the gateway to Dovedale and a starting point for those wanting to visit Izaak Walton country

The church of St Oswald, described by the author George Eliot as 'the finest mere parish church in the Kingdom', features a 212ft (67m) high spire, and is still regarded as one of the grandest sights in Derbyshire. The church is connected to the market square by Church Street, an eye-catching thoroughfare containing a wealth of interesting architecture, including the Queen Elizabeth Grammar School (right), as well some fine Georgian houses and almshouses.

In 1745, having defeated the British at Prestonpans, Charles Edward Stuart, commonly known as Bonnie Prince Charlie, advanced to Derby. While camped at Ashbourne in December 1745, he declared James, his father, King of England,

At Ashbourne on December 3rd 1745, Charles Edward Stuart declared his father James King of England, Wales and Scotland.

Wales and Scotland; a plaque in the marketplace commemorates this event. The famous pub sign for the Green Man and Black Head Hotel straddles Church Street at the town end, and features in the *Guinness Book of Records* as the longest pub sign in the world. James Boswell and Dr Johnson visited the Green Man while staying at the 17th century Mansion House on Church Street, and Queen Victoria, while still a young princess, called in for tea.

Ashbourne is famous, or notorious, for the annual Royal Shrovetide football game, played on Shrove Tuesday and Ash Wednesday, although it resembles a re-enactment of the civil war rather than a sporting event! The game is contested by two huge teams, formed by those born on the north side of the river Henmore versus those born on the south side. The game was given its royal title after being started, or 'turned up', by the then Prince of Wales in 1928; in 2003 HRH Prince Charles started the match.

ASHFORD-IN-THE-WATER

*Two miles north-west of Bakewell, just off the busy A6, the idyllic village of Ashford-in-the-Water
sits on the river Wye, crossed by the three arches of medieval Sheepwash Bridge*

Most of the beautiful limestone cottages gathered round the church of the Holy Trinity in Ashford date back to the late 18th and early 19th centuries. The abundance of water in the village is the inspiration for the six well-dressings which take place every June and attract thousands of visitors. The custom was revived fairly recently after decades of decline.

Although lead was mined in the area until the late 19th century, Ashford is most famous for the so-called Black Marble, an impure form of limestone which turns black when polished. First quarried in 1748 by Henry Watson, the black marble was loved by the Victorians who used it in fireplaces, vases and jewellery. It was exported all over the world; some fine examples can be seen in the church of the Holy Trinity.

BAKEWELL

A thriving Derbyshire market town on the eastern edge of the Peak District National Park, Bakewell is known as the 'Capital of the Peak'

The ancient five-arched bridge crossing the river Wye at Bakewell dates back to the 13th century, and is still open to traffic to this day. Another ancient packhorse bridge lies further upstream. In the mid 19th century, a cook at the Rutland Arms mis-read a recipe for jam tarts, putting the jam mixture in first, accidentally creating the town's most famous export, the Bakewell pudding or tart. Forty years earlier, Jane Austen is reputed to have stayed at the same hotel while writing *Pride and Prejudice*.

BALLIDON

Located five miles north of Ashbourne in the White Peak, Ballidon is an isolated spot which in 2001 had a population of 79

A lonely hamlet in the Derbyshire Dales, Ballidon was once a thriving medieval settlement but all that remains now are some farms gathered near a large limestone quarry, and a tiny isolated 17th century chapel, Ballidon All Saints, which literally stands in a field.

BAMFORD

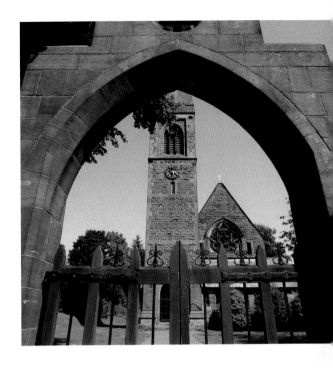

Nestling beneath the cliffs of Bamford Edge, the village of Bamford occupies a delightful position on the banks of the river Derwent close to the dams of the Upper Derwent valley

The 18th century cotton mill closed down in the 1960s and, like many former Peak District mills, now houses modern apartments. The mill wheel survives, and the adjoining mill pool is one of the prettiest spots along the Derwent. The church of St John the Baptist has an interesting design, featuring a very sharp spire and slim tower.

BASLOW

North of the Chatsworth Park estate on the river Derwent, the village of Baslow is divided into three distinct parts: Over End, Nether End and Bridge End

The three arches of the 17th century bridge complete with its small stone guardhouse for the toll-collector span the river Derwent at Bridge End, the oldest part of the village. Further up the Derwent at nearby Calver, the seven-storey former mill dating back to the 18th century has now been converted into apartments, but in the 1970s it was used as the setting for Colditz Castle in the television series. North of the villages, the edges of Curbar and Baslow form a rocky escarpment with glorious views over the Derwent valley. In a local custom, the 20ft (6m) Eagle Rock on Baslow Edge must be climbed by the menfolk of Baslow before they are considered worthy of marriage!

BEELEY

Six miles north of Matlock, the Chatsworth estate village of Beeley is a small collection of gritstone cottages housing estate workers

In 1747 the Duke of Devonshire purchased Beeley Hill as part of a grand plan to landscape the Chatsworth estate. The village remains much as it was over 200 years ago with houses built of honey-coloured sandstone quarried locally close to Fallinge Edge. Parts of the church of St Anne's date back to the 14th century, and the church retains a Norman doorway, although much of the existing building is the result of Victorian restoration.

BIRCHOVER

Five miles north-west of Matlock, on a
hillside rising to Stanton Moor, stands the
village of Birchover, consisting mainly of
17th and 18th century gritstone cottages

Behind the Druid Inn lies Rowtor Rocks, a small
gritstone tor, which was said to have been used by
Druids to perform magical rites. The Reverend
Thomas Eyre carved a cave out of the rocks, complete
with steps and seats for himself and his friends to
sit and admire the view – now sadly obscured by trees.
The Red Lion pub has the unusual distinction of
having a 30ft (9m) well in the bar. At the top of the
village is a huge stonecutting works and behind are
some large quarries where gritstone is still extracted.

BRADFIELD

To the north-west of Sheffield, this Yorkshire Peak village is divided into Low Bradfield and High Bradfield. The church of St Nicholas stands at 860ft (262m) above sea level

Low Bradfield was largely destroyed in the great Sheffield flood of 1864 but High Bradfield offers spectacular views over the Loxley valley. The topiary adorns part of the old Work House, built in 1769 to house the poor and homeless of the parish. Further up the hill stands the old post office and the Watch House, built in 1745 to prevent bodysnatching from the churchyard.

BRASSINGTON

At the south-eastern corner of the Peak District,
between Wirksworth and Ashbourne,
lies the picturesque village of Brassington

Now a quiet place, Brassington was once a thriving centre for the local leadmining industry. The village is situated on a limestone plateau 800ft (240m) above sea level and the area around is marked by the tell-tale hillocks and mounds of hundreds of long-since abandoned mines; in places, there is evidence of old miners' buildings. Most of the village cottages are constructed using local limestone and some date back to the 17th and 18th centuries. One of the oldest, inappropriately named the Tudor House, dates from 1615. Close to the village are the strange rock formations of Rainster Rocks, the site of a Roman settlement, and Hipley Hill. Brassington appears in the Domesday Book as Branzingtune.

BUXTON

Standing at a height of 1,000ft (305m) above sea level, Buxton proudly claims the title of the highest town in England. It is situated in a natural bowl amongst the surrounding Derbyshire hills, where the gritstone of the north peak gives way to the limestone of the south

Buxton has been famous for its thermal spa waters since the time of the Romans, who built baths here in the first century AD. The famous spring of St Ann's Well is next to the magnificent Crescent (far left), commissioned by the 5th Duke of Devonshire in 1780, and completed 10 years later, using locally quarried gritstone. The Pavilion Gardens (below, left and centre) stand on the banks of the river Wye and were opened in 1871. They house the spa-water swimming pool and the Victorian pavilion – a conservatory containing many exotic and tropical plants. The main shopping area in Buxton is Spring Gardens, pictured left.

CASTLETON

At the western end of the Hope valley, the picturesque village of Castleton is surrounded on three sides by the looming hills of Mam Tor, Hollins Cross and Lose Hill

One of the most popular destinations in the Peak District, Castleton has much to offer the visitor: a castle, beautiful walking country and, close by, the four show caverns of Speedwell, Blue John, Treak Cliff and Peak Cavern – otherwise known as the Devil's Arse! Peak Cavern is the source of the small river known as Peakshole Water which winds its way through the oldest part of the village. Following the Limestone Way out of Castleton, rugged Cave Dale, pictured left, climbs to offer spectacular views back to the village and Lose Hill.

Peveril Castle watches over Castleton from its lofty vantage point above Cave Dale. It was built in Norman times for William Peveril, the son of William the Conqueror, who the king appointed as royal bailiff to oversee north-west Derbyshire. Further additions to the castle were made right up to the 19th century. Hollins Cross is visible on the skyline, on the ridge leading from Mam Tor to Lose Hill.

Starting in the village is an enjoyable, though strenuous, 6.5 mile (10km) walk that takes the rambler across the Hope Valley to Lose Hill. From the summit a paved path leads to Mam Tor, sometimes known as the 'Shivering Mountain' due to the unstable rocks from which it is formed.

CHAPEL-EN-LE-FRITH

*The name Chapel-en-le-Frith refers to
a church built by foresters from the
Royal Forest in 1225, 'frith' being an old
Norman French word meaning forest*

The busy market town of Chapel-en-le-Frith stands 776ft (237m) above sea level, just off the A6 between Stockport and Buxton. The cobbled marketplace contains stocks dating back to the Cromwellian period and a market cross, pictured here. On the right is Church Brow, a very steep cobbled street leading down from Market Street to the High Street, full of quaint stone cottages. As well as the annual well dressing, Chapel holds a Scarecrow Festival, in which weird and wonderful figures appear all over the village to surprise the unwary visitor!

CHELMORTON

Set in the midst of an area of limestone quarrying, Chelmorton is a classic example of a linear Peak District village

Situated four miles south-east of Buxton, Chelmorton is 1,200ft (366m) above sea level and is the highest village in Derbyshire. The steep hill of Chelmorton Low looms above the village, from which a stream flows down, bearing the name of Illy Willy Water.

The church of St John the Baptist is Derbyshire's highest church. It partly dates back to Norman times, although the spire was added to the 13th century tower in the 15th century. Chelmorton retains many medieval strip farms in the fields around the village; some of the 13 surviving strips are visible in the photograph on the left. Many of the farm buildings along the main street are built from local limestone.

CRESSBROOK

*Sited amongst magnificent scenery, Cressbrook, once a busy mill village,
is now a quiet backwater on the river Wye. It lies close to the river gorge of
Water-cum-Jolly and upstream from Monsal Head*

The lofty crag of Peter's Stone stands guard over Cressbrook Dale, a beautiful gorge-like limestone dale, north of the village of Cressbrook. Cressbrook Mill, now converted into apartments after becoming derelict, was built in 1815 on the site of the original mill owned by Richard Arkwright. The attractive cottages at the top of the hill were built in the 19th century as a model village to house workers at the mill. Some of the mill-workers were orphaned children who were brought from London by the manager William Newton. Known as the Minstrel of the Peak, Newton had been sacked 25 years earlier by Richard Arkwright.

CROMFORD

Cromford is sometimes called the cradle of the industrial revolution, thanks to the legacy of Richard Arkwright, the famous mill-owner who built the first successful watermill here in 1771. The buildings at Cromford now form part of the Derwent Valley Mills World Heritage Site

Before the arrival of Arkwright, Cromford was a small settlement consisting of a few cottages and a chapel, gathered around a packhorse bridge. After building his cotton mill, Arkwright also built cottages for the workers, a corn mill, the Greyhound Hotel, and established a market. The three-storey houses on North Street are considered among the finest surviving examples of industrial architecture. The large pond behind the Greyhound, with North Street behind, now serves as a duck pond, but originally held water from Bonsal brook to supply a head of water for the mills.

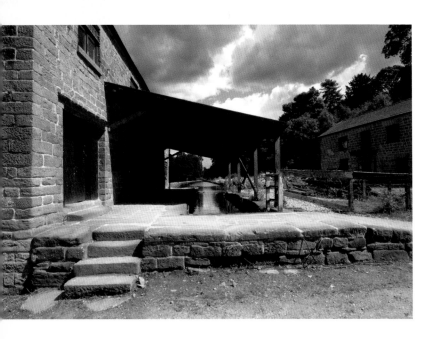

The Cromford canal was built in the 1790s to improve the movement of goods in and out of Cromford and linked with the Erewash canal in Nottingham, eventually reaching the river Trent. Plans to link the canal to the Peak Forest canal at Whaley Bridge were abandoned because of the prohibitive cost of cutting through the Derbyshire hills, and the Cromford and High Peak Railway was built instead. Its track bed now serves as a footpath and bridleway called the High Peak Trail.

Traces of Richard Arkwright's legacy are visible all around the village, and include canal buildings (left), historic shops (below) and workers' cottages (right). Cromford's mill-workers came from all over the country; he preferred weavers with large families – the women and children labouring in the spinning factory and the men toiling at home, turning the yarn into cloth.

EDALE

The village of Edale is really a collection of five smaller hamlets: Nether Booth, Ollerbooth, Upper Booth, Barber Booth and Grindsbrook Booth of which the village called Edale is part

Edale nestles below the upland moorland plateau of Kinder Scout and marks the beginning of the Pennine Way, Britain's first long-distance footpath which continues for 250 miles (400km) northwards before its finish at Kirk Yetholm on the Scottish border. By tradition, the last stop before embarking on the walk is to call in at the Old Nags Head pub (right), the official starting point.

From Edale, the Pennine Way winds through Grindsbrook Clough before climbing to Kinder Scout, which at 2,088ft (636m), is the highest point in Derbyshire – although an alternative route goes via Jacobs Ladder from Upper Booth.

In the Middle Ages, Edale valley was a royal forest where farming and settlements were discouraged because they interrupted hunting. This meant that Edale was a relatively quiet spot until Tudor times when the royal forest system collapsed. The village developed slowly, but was given a massive boost in 1894 when the railway which linked Manchester to Sheffield arrived. At a very early stage, Edale became an idyllic commuter village for the two cities on its doorstep. The railway also brought thousands of walkers, delighted to swap the hustle and bustle of city life for the wide open spaces at the weekend.

KINDER SCOUT

The vast, brooding area of moorland known as Kinder Scout dominates the northern part of the Peak District and is a magnet for walkers

Kinder Scout lies between the villages of Edale and Hayfield. The large windswept plateau – the highest in the Peaks – rises sharply from the surrounding countryside and is studded with rocky outcrops (left). The escarpment at the western edge of Kinder, and Kinder Downfall which drains most of the water from the plateau, are particular favourites with walkers.

Here and there can be found the scattered wreckage of aircraft (below) many of which came to grief during the Second World War when bombers returning from night raids would become lost over the dark landscape.

Below the Downfall, the river Kinder flows into the beautiful Kinder Reservoir (right), on the western flank of Kinder Scout.

EDENSOR

The small village of Edensor – pronounced 'Ensor' – is set within the beautiful parkland of the Chatsworth estate; it was relocated by the 4th Duke of Devonshire so that it would not be seen from Chatsworth House

St Peter's Church was designed by the great Victorian church architect Sir George Gilbert Scott and built in 1870 on the site of the previous 14th century church. Joseph Paxton, designer of the Crystal Palace and the head gardener of the 6th Duke of Devonshire, is buried in the churchyard, along with Kathleen Kennedy, married to the 10th Duke's eldest son and sister of President John F Kennedy, who visited the area shortly before his death in 1963. Chatsworth House, originally built by Bess of Hardwick, was used in the 2005 film of the Jane Austen novel *Pride and Prejudice* as the setting for Pemberley, the home of Mr Darcy.

ELTON

Perched on an exposed hillside, Elton stands on the southern edge of the White Peak limestone plateau, overlooking Stanton-in-the-Peak and Youlgrave

The 17th and 18th century sandstone cottages of Elton were once occupied by workers in the nearby leadmines and evidence of mining is still visible in the area. Elton is popular with walkers, who are attracted by the strange collection of rocks known as Robin Hood's Stride, otherwise known as Mock Beggar Hall, and the medieval cave underneath Cratcliffe Rocks. Four large standing stones are all that remain of a much larger stone circle: the remaining stones were pillaged to construct local walls and buildings.

EYAM

Eyam will forever be known as the 'plague village', whose inhabitants bravely isolated themselves in 1665 to prevent the disease from spreading further after many of the villagers became infected

The plague first appeared in Eyam in the house now known as the Plague Cottage, pictured right, then occupied by a travelling tailor, who inadvertently introduced the plague to Eyam in a parcel of flea-infested cloth from London. The rector of Eyam, William Mompesson, persuaded most of the inhabitants to stay and seal off the village, even though many died from the disease. The church of St Lawrence contains several artefacts dating back to the plague, including Mompesson's chair, and the churchyard is the resting place for many of the victims, including Mompesson's wife Catherine. Eyam Hall, pictured far left, is a 17th century manor house, built in 1676, and has been the home of the Wright family ever since.

From the rear of the church, a footpath leads to Mompessons Well, a spring covered by a gritstone slab, pictured above. Food and provisions were put here by people from neighbouring villages, in return for money left by the people of Eyam, who disinfected the coins in vinegar. The plague lasted 16 months in Eyam, and killed at least 260 villagers, about half the population. To prevent the spread of the disease, the church was closed during the outbreak and services were held in Cucklett Delph, a small valley nearby. Commemorative services are still held there annually.

GLOSSOP

There are two Glossops – the bustling
market town on the main A57 road from
Manchester to Sheffield, and Old Glossop,
a collection of older buildings gathered
round the parish church

Situated in the far north-west of Derbyshire, just
outside the boundaries of the Peak District National
Park, Glossop was settled by the Romans in the first
century AD, and a Roman road known as Doctor's
Gate leads from Old Glossop to the slopes of
Bleaklow, high up on the Snake Pass. The new town
was mostly built in the 19th century, centred around
the town hall, and originally named Howard Town,
before acquiring the name Glossop from the ancient
village settlement now known as Old Glossop.

Old Glossop features several 17th and 18th century
cottages clustered around the Norman church, and
standing opposite is a fine old 13th century carved
stone cross, although the top is a 20th century

addition, marking the coronation of George V in 1910. The village expanded rapidly during the 16th and 17th centuries, as the wool and cotton industries developed, and the cottages pictured above would have been occupied by weavers. After the arrival of Arkwright's water-powered cotton mills, Glossop expanded again, the population multiplying six times in less than 50 years.

At the top of Norfolk Square, facing the town hall, is Glossop Heritage Centre, which has a permanent exhibition illustrating the area's fascinating history plus a large archive of local photographs, maps and other historic material.

GREAT LONGSTONE

The twin villages of Great and Little Longstone sit beneath Longstone Edge, a high gritstone ridge sadly disfigured by lead and fluorspar quarrying

Great Longstone is a picturesque limestone village two miles north of Bakewell, sheltering beneath the five-mile Longstone Edge, where the lead was found which brought the village its early prosperity. Flowers now bloom in the trough below the last surviving of the two village water pumps. The water was condemned in 1895 as unfit for human consumption but the well continued to supply the village with water for another seven years. The medieval cross standing on the village green dates back to a time when Great Longstone had a flourishing weaving and shoe-making industry, whose patron saint Crispin is commemorated in the adjacent Crispin Inn.

St Giles Church, hidden away at the end of the village, dates back to the 13th century. Further additions were made in the 14th and 15th centuries, including a fine beamed roof, before a large-scale restoration was carried out in 1872 by the eminent London architect Richard Norman Shaw. This fine church also serves the neighbouring villages of Hassop, Rowland, Wardlow and Little Longstone. Inside there is a memorial to Dr Edward Buxton who, in the early part of the 19th century, tended the village during an outbreak of typhus.

HARTINGTON

One of the most beautiful villages in Derbyshire, historic Hartington on the river Dove is a popular tourist spot in the Peak District

Hartington possesses all the elements necessary for a picturesque village – a marketplace, village green, duck pond, 17th century hall, fine old church, limestone cottages and even a cheese factory! The market charter was granted in 1203, although a market has not been held here for many years. The parish church of St Giles stands above the village and was largely constructed of sandstone during the 14th and 15th centuries. It has a perpendicular west tower with battlements.

North of the village is Long Dale, pictured far left, a deserted limestone dale three miles long. Hartington Hall (left), a magnificent 17th century Tudor manor house where Bonnie Prince Charlie once spent a night, is now a youth hostel. Built in 1611 for Thomas Bateman, it remained in the Bateman family for centuries until it was sold to the YHA in 1948. Retaining its country house atmosphere, it is now one of the association's most luxurious properties.

Hartington is justly famous for Nuttall's Creamery, pictured top right, which manufactures one quarter of the world's supply of Stilton cheese, along with the less well-known Buxton Blue. The cheese factory originally opened in 1870 and is now the only survivor of the seven cheese factories originally in the area. The Old Cheese Shop, in the village, sells the classic Blue Stilton as well as regional favourites such as Buxton Blue and Dovedale.

HASSOP

Three miles north of Bakewell, the tiny village of Hassop grew up around the local leadmining industry which proliferated until the mid 19th century

The imposing Hassop Hall was rebuilt in its current form in the early 17th century on the site of a much older house by the landowning Eyre family, whose wealth came from leadmining. Legend has it that a secret entrance to an old leadmine still exists under a manhole hidden in the cellar.

The Eyres were a devout Jacobean family and steadfast Roman Catholics, and during the Civil War of 1643 the hall was established as a Royalist garrison by Rowland Eyre. Several skirmishes took place and, following the Parliamentary victory, the captured hall was redeemed by the family who had to pay £21,000 for the privilege – a massive sum at the time. All Saints church (right) was built by the Eyres in the Classical style in 1818 and is connected to the hall by an underground passage.

Hassop Hall is now an elegant hotel and is a popular venue for weddings.

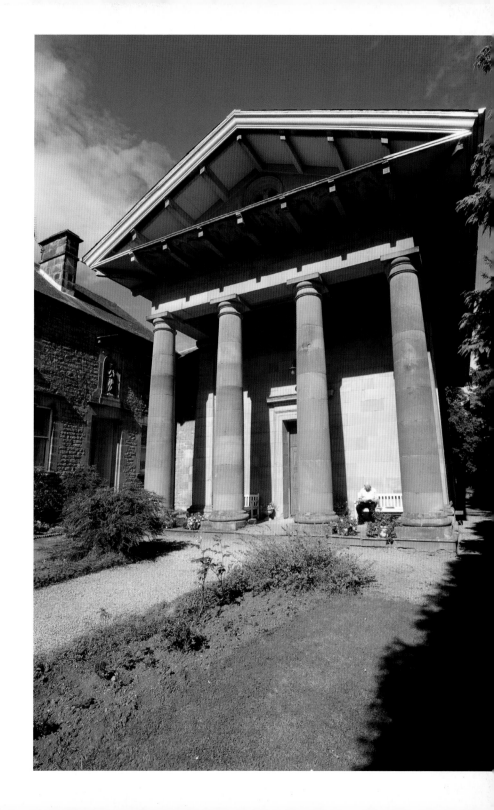

HATHERSAGE

On the banks of the river Derwent, ten miles west of Sheffield, Hathersage
is a large gritstone village surrounded by wild moorland

Standing on a crossroads near the border with South Yorkshire, Hathersage is now an attractive village popular with walkers and climbers. But in Victorian times this was a grim mill town, where five chimneys belched out choking black smoke and working conditions were so bad that life expectancy was no greater than 30 years. By the mid 18th century, Hathersage had become famous for its brass buttons and was the centre of the wire, pin, and needle industry, but it declined in the early years of the 20th century when nearby Sheffield developed more advanced machinery.

Hathersage has several interesting historical connections. Charlotte Bronte stayed at the vicarage while writing *Jane Eyre*, whose name she borrowed from the well-known Derbyshire family. In the novel, Hathersage appears as Norton. Hathersage is probably best-known as the supposed last resting place of Little John, Robin Hood's trusted deputy. St Michael's churchyard contains the 10ft long grave. It was dug up in 1784 by James Shuttleworth and a 30in (762mm) thigh bone was uncovered. A bone of this length indicates that its owner was between seven (2.1m) and eight feet (2.4 m) tall.

HAYFIELD

Overlooked by the bulk of Kinder Scout, Hayfield sits on the river Sett in the High Peak, on a Roman road and an old packhorse route between Yorkshire and Cheshire

The 17th century cottages at the heart of Hayfield testify to the age of the village. These three-storey weavers' cottages appeared when Hayfield expanded with the arrival of the cotton and wool-spinning industries. The industry was in decline by the mid 1800s, and now the principal business of Hayfield is dealing with the large numbers of visitors who set off up Kinder Scout, retracing the footsteps of the participants of the 1932 Mass Trespass.

In April of that year hundreds of ramblers set out from Bowden Bridge, where the river Sett meets the Kinder, and challenged the authority of the landowners by walking up onto Kinder Scout. A small group of game-keepers tried in vain to block their route but the marchers continued up to Ashop Head where they held a public meeting before returning to Hayfield. Their triumph was shortlived, however, as a number of policemen awaited their return and arrested five of the party. Several were arrested and some received gaol sentences of 18 months.

HOPE

At the confluence of Peakshole Water and the river Noe, Hope stands in the Hope Valley, below Win Hill and Lose Hill, close to the Roman settlement known as Navio

The stump of the Saxon cross in the churchyard of St Peter is proof of the antiquity of the village, which is recorded in the Domesday Book as one of the earliest centres of Christianity in the area. The church dates back to the 14th century and features the carving of a Celtic face on the side of the tower.

Hope is justly famous for the craftsmanship and ingenuity of its annual well dressings, which take place in July. These beautiful decorations are made by covering large boards with damp clay and then attaching petals, bark and other natural objects to make an attractive picture.

The figure of the climber scaling the west face of Old Hall Cottage represents the Yorkshire mountaineer Alan Hinkes, who in 2005 completed ascents of all 14 of the world's 8,000m peaks, the first Briton to achieve this feat.

ILAM

Visitors to Dovedale usually call at the pretty village of Ilam, tucked away at the lower end of the river Manifold. The river often disappears below ground and only emerges in very wet weather

The unusual appearance of Ilam is due to the industrialist Jesse Watts-Russell who rebuilt most of the cottages in the 1820s in a distinctive Alpine style – very different from the grand Ilam Hall, which was re-designed by the architect John Shaw with battlements, towers and chimneys. Leaving the village, first Bunster Hill then Thorpe Cloud stand guard over the entrance to Dovedale, close to the Izaak Walton Hotel, named in remembrance of the author of *The Compleat Angler* who will forever be associated with Dovedale. The photograph shows walkers entering the rocky gorge as the river Dove winds around Thorpe Cloud on the right.

LITTLE HUCKLOW

The tiny hamlet of Little Hucklow lies three miles north of Tideswell in the High Peak, in an area where leadmining was the principal industry

The ancient village of Little Hucklow, high on the Derbyshire moors, consists mainly of limestone cottages and farm buildings. The village pub, the Olde Bull's Head, dates from the 12th century and claims to be the fifth oldest pub in England. Little Hucklow retains much evidence of its historic leadmining past with several old mineshafts and gravel hillocks visible around the village.

LONGNOR

Situated just over the border in Staffordshire, Longnor lies on the north bank of the river Manifold, close to the river Dove. The television series Peak Practice is filmed here

The cobbled market square and the quaint network of cobbled lanes that wind around the village give Longnor a unique character all of its own. The old Victorian market hall, pictured far left, dates from 1873 and displays a list of tariffs for making sales above the entrance; it is now a craft centre. The church of St Bartholomew has roots which go back 800 years, although the present building was constructed in the 18th century. The building is not considered to be very attractive and is best known for the tomb of William Billinge who was born in a cornfield in 1679, lived through the reign of seven monarchs, fought in several wars, and died in Longnor aged 112.

Above and left: with its quaint cobbled lanes and market square, Longnor is the setting for the television series *Peak Practice*

MATLOCK

The twin towns of Matlock and Matlock Bath are located on the A6 in the east of Derbyshire, just outside the boundary of the Peak District National Park

Matlock is the county town of Derbyshire but was an unimportant collection of small villages until the discovery of the warm springs in 1698. John Smedley, the pioneer of hydrotherapy, built the vast hydro in 1853 and another 20 hydros were soon in operation locally. Smedley's Hydro, the large building in the photograph on the right, continued as a bath house until the 1950s when it became the offices of Derbyshire County Council. The redbrick Victorian houses of Matlock contrast with the whitewashed cottages of Matlock Bath, photographed left, which seem to cling to the hillside below the Heights of Abraham. Smedley also built Riber Castle, a large folly now in ruins but at one time a wildlife centre for endangered species.

MATLOCK BATH

Lying in a wooded valley one mile south of Matlock, the spa town of Matlock Bath became a fashionable resort during the Victorian era

On the banks of the river Derwent, Matlock Bath, dubbed 'Little Switzerland' by Lord Byron, was transformed in the 1840s by the arrival of the railway, allowing day-trippers from all over the midlands to visit. There are breathtaking views from the Heights of Abraham above Matlock Bath; the quickest way up is to take the cable car (left), which was built in 1984 and is Britain's first alpine cable car system.

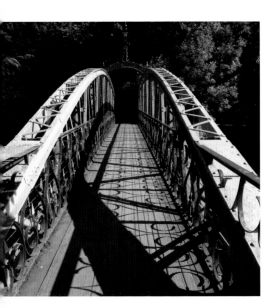

Top: cable cars transport visitors high above the dizzying Heights of Abraham; *above*: the arch of the pedestrian bridge over the river Derwent

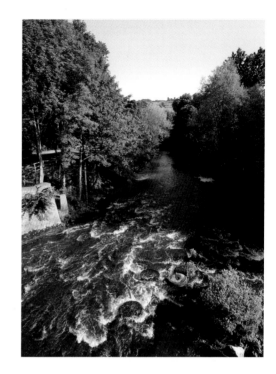

Masson Mills, built in 1873 and in continuous use until 1991, is the finest surviving example of Sir Richard Arkwright's cotton mills and retains working textile machinery. The building is renowned for its elegant architecture, with Venetian windows and a cupola above the bay containing a bell which summoned the millworkers each day.

The Venetian theme appears again in Matlock Bath's most well-known event, the Illuminations and Venetian Nights. Held every autumn, the cliffs are illuminated and a clifftop firework display is held. Decorated boats sail down the river Derwent in a procession of light originally devised to celebrate Queen Victoria's Diamond Jubilee.

MIDDLETON-BY-YOULGREAVE

*A quiet leafy village a mile from Youlgrave,
Middleton sits by the river Bradford about six miles
south of Bakewell, near the Arbor Low stone circle*

An attractive collection of stone cottages and farms, Middleton has some interesting historical connections. Nothing now remains of the manor house once owned by the Fulwood family, except for a mound and the remains of a wall, but during the English Civil War Sir Christopher Fulwood was shot after organising a local force in support of the king.

Dating from 2500BC, Arbor Low (far left) is the most important stone circle in the north of England, and like Stonehenge, its purpose is still being debated. It consists of 46 large stones and 13 smaller stones. Its origins are shrouded in mystery and it is not known why the stones lie flat – they could have been placed in this way, or it is possible that they were upright and toppled over at a later date.

MONSAL DALE

The view of the river Wye winding through Upperdale and Monsal Dale from Monsal Head is one of the most beautiful vistas in the Peak District

'The valley is gone – and now every fool in Buxton can be in Bakewell in half an hour and every fool at Bakewell in Buxton' – this was the reaction of the critic John Ruskin, who campaigned against the construction in 1863 of the viaduct across the river Wye at Monsal Dale, a horseshoe-shaped valley viewed from the lofty vantage point of Monsal Head.

The Midland railway line which crossed the viaduct was closed for good in the 1960s, and the bridge is now part of the Monsal Trail, an eight-mile walking route established by the Peak District National Park. The railway originally continued under Monsal Head via a series of tunnels but these are now closed for safety reasons. Interestingly, the viaduct that excited so much opposition when built now seems to blend quite naturally with the dale.

MONYASH

*Five miles north-west of
Bakewell, Monyash's limestone
cottages cluster around the
village green, near the head
of Lathkill Dale*

The beautiful, ancient farming village of
Monyash is sited on a bed of impervious clay,
which originally held five stretches of water
known as 'meres' fed by underground
springs. Just one remains, Fere Mere,
pictured right, once the source of the village
drinking water. As the centre for leadmining
in the White Peak, Monyash held a Barmote
Court which sat twice a year to settle mining
disputes. Monyash became a market town
in 1340 and the old market cross still stands
on the village green. The adjacent hamlet
of Over Haddon leads down to the glorious
scenery of Lathkill Dale, which starts at
Monyash as a dry riverbed but becomes a
river about a mile down the valley where a
spring emerges from a cave.

The 12th century church of St Leonard
retains some Norman features and contains
a chest which dates back to the 13th century.

PARWICH

In a peaceful setting, situated on high hills, Parwich is a very attractive village on the southern fringe of the Peak District National Park in the Derbyshire Dales

The limestone cottages of Parwich are gathered around the village green and duck pond in picturesque fashion, and in summer the pretty gardens are alive with colour. Although quite close to Dovedale in the west, the village benefits from its location off the beaten track, away from the major tourist routes and destinations.

The church of St Peter appears to be Norman but is in fact Victorian, and was built in 1873; the previous church had occupied the site for 800 years. Next to the church gate stands a beautiful limestone Celtic cross which serves as the village war memorial and honours the memory of the men who fought and died in two world wars.

Next to the Dam, once a sheep dip but now home to the village ducks, stands the Sycamore Inn which dates back to the 17th century. Although much of Parwich is not particularly ancient, there is evidence of a Roman field system and manor house, as well as later medieval buildings, which can be viewed as part of a heritage walk.

ROWSLEY

Rowsley is a village of two halves, standing at the confluence of the rivers Wye and Derwent, five miles from Bakewell

Greater Rowsley is the original settlement, positioned at the river junction. Little Rowsley developed as a result of the arrival of the Midland Railway line and the construction of the station, designed by Joseph Paxton in 1849. Disputes with the Dukes of Rutland and Devonshire delayed construction of the railway as the dukes initially refused to allow the line to cross their estates of Haddon and Chatsworth. Eventually, the Duke of Rutland relented, and the line finally reached Manchester in 1867. The arrival of the railway led to the development of a separate railway village, which is now the site of an engineering works.

The Peacock Hotel was built in 1652 by John Stevenson, whose inscription appears above the door. A superb ceramic peacock perches haughtily on the balustrade above the signboard, the emblem of the Manners family, owners of nearby Haddon Hall.

Caudwell's Mill was built in 1874, replacing a previous structure over 400 years old, and is now the last remaining water turbine-powered flour mill in the country. After closing in 1978, an energetic local campaign got it re-opened and it is now open to the public and continues to mill a small amount of flour.

SHELDON

A stone's throw from Bakewell, Sheldon was once the centre of a thriving leadmining area where rival gangs competed ruthlessly for the best veins of ore; today it is a sleepy village of stone cottages and farms

The stone cottages of Sheldon mostly date back to the 18th century, when leadmining was active in the area. Apart from farm buildings, there is a pub, the Cock and Pullet, and the small parish church of St Michael and All Angels, built in the 19th century using material from the previous church.

Half a mile south of the village, the Magpie Mine is one of the best-preserved leadmines in Britain. Featuring a distinctive Cornish-style engine house and chimney, the mine was finally closed in 1924. It operated for 300 years, despite repeated problems with flooding in its 728ft (222m) shaft. The mine was the scene of the notorious Magpie Murders in 1833, when three miners were killed by fires started deliberately by a rival gang in a dispute over ownership of a rich vein of lead ore. Rumour has it that the widows of the dead miners cursed the mine and their ghosts are said to haunt the old workings.

Today, many relics of the mine's former glory remain, including the engine house, the ore-crushing circle and the drainage ditch.

STANTON-IN-THE-PEAK

The village of Stanton-in-the-Peak lies along a steep twisting lane below the mysterious Stanton Moor, where the Nine Ladies Stone Circle and other prehistoric sites can be found

The estate village of Stanton-in-the-Peak was built during the 18th and 19th centuries by the Thornhill family. The initials WPT, which appear above the doorway of the Flying Childers pub, and several cottages, belong to William Paul Thornhill of nearby Stanton Hall. The Flying Childers was a racehorse owned by the Duke of Devonshire in the 1700s. He was never beaten, and his portrait still hangs at Chatsworth Hall, where he retired. Holly House, pictured far right, had eight of its 14 windows blocked, to avoid the window tax of 1697.

TADDINGTON

Standing on a high limestone ridge north-west of Bakewell, the tiny hamlet of Taddington is close to several interesting prehistoric burial sites

The little village of Taddington is arranged in linear fashion along a single lane, consisting mostly of limestone cottages and farm buildings. The parish church of St Michael mostly dates back to the 14th century but was extensively restored in the 19th century. The most important local ancient site is the Five Wells Tumulus, from which 12 burials were excavated by Thomas Bateman in 1846.

TIDESWELL

Six miles east of Buxton, Tideswell is the home of 'the Cathedral of the Peak', the magnificent 14th century church of St John the Baptist

Situated on the river Wye, Tideswell is one of the Peak District's most ancient settlements. It dates back to pre-Roman times and was granted its market charter in 1251. The magnificent church, considered to be the finest in the Peak District, was completed in 1400 and replaced a smaller Norman church on the same site. It was built by Sir John Foljambe, a member of the well-known Derbyshire landowning family. Like many other Peak District villages, the prosperity of Tideswell was first founded on leadmining. Then, in the 19th century, it became a centre for the textile industry, producing both cotton and silk goods.

TINTWISTLE

The Peak District National Park boundary neatly bisects the small village of Tintwistle, at the foot of the Longdendale valley three miles north of Glossop

Tintwistle and the neighbouring village of Woodhead are surrounded by a series of reservoirs built to supply water to the city of Manchester. In 1848 the Woodhead reservoir was constructed and others quickly followed. The two closest to Tintwistle are Bottoms and Arnfield which is situated to the west of the village. Tintwistle Well Dressing takes place in the last week of June, and in 2005 celebrated the fiftieth anniversary of VE Day.

TISSINGTON

In the south-east corner of the Derbyshire Dales, five miles north of Ashbourne, the estate village of Tissington grew up around Tissington Hall, home of the FitzHerbert family for over 400 years

After over 650 years of well-dressing, Tissington claims to be the original home of this unusual festival, although there are various competing claims from other Peak settlements! The photograph (top left) shows Town Well, one of six wells in the village. The village is set back from the main Ashbourne to Buxton road in an idyllic setting dominated by the Jacobean Tissington Hall which was built by Francis FitzHerbert in 1609 and extended several times over the centuries by his descendants.

Entered from the main road through a set of fine gates, Tissington consists of limestone cottages and other buildings, including the Old School House, pictured bottom left, now a kindergarten. The village developed in haphazard fashion, with no overall design and this undoubtedly contributes to its charm. The Old Kitchen Garden still stands behind the duck pond and one of the cottages houses a candle workshop.

The old railway line from Ashbourne to Buxton has been transformed into the 13 mile (21km) long Tissington Trail, popular with walkers and cyclists alike. At Parsley Hay the trail links with the High Peak Trail. Both trails were originally part of the Buxton to Ashbourne railway line which was built in 1899 and operated until 1967.

Left and above: the magnificent Tissington Hall; its coach house, which serves as a tea room, won an award for 'the best conversion of a redundant building in the east of England'

UPPERDALE

The river Wye winds through Chee Dale and Millers Dale before passing below Upperdale bridge, close to the tiny hamlet of Upperdale and Monsal Head in some of the most superb limestone scenery in the Peak District

The banks of the river Wye at Upperdale are sublimely peaceful. The river is famous for a unique variety of rainbow trout, as well as the more common brown trout, both of which reach impressive proportions thanks to the rich cocktail of nutrients generated by the abundant local limestone. This stretch of the river is owned by the Chatsworth estate, and fly fishing permits can be purchased from the Monsal Dale river-keeper. The bridge provides a useful viewpoint over the river, as wading is not permitted.

The river Wye is one of three Derbyshire rivers that rise on Axe Edge Moor above Buxton; the other two are the Manifold and the Dove. The Wye eventually meets the Derwent at Rowsley, before finally joining the river Trent in Nottinghamshire. The water around Upperdale is generally very clear, since it is filtered through the limestone, although fishermen claim this just makes it easier for the fish to spot them!

WILDBOARCLOUGH

*In the county of Cheshire, close to Macclesfield, Wildboarclough sits at
the foot of Shutingsloe, known rather fancifully as the Cheshire Matterhorn,
due to a supposed similarity in shape to its Alpine cousin*

Wildboarclough, at the north-west extremity of the Peak District National Park, is said to be the site of the slaying of England's last wild boar. Little remains of the mills once powered by the waters of Clough brook; however, the Mill House, the imposing building pictured right, formerly the administration block of a carpet mill, later had the distinction of becoming the largest sub post office in the country.

In 1989, a flash flood occurred which tragically killed a motorist, and swamped the Edinboro Cottages, pictured below centre. The Cat and Fiddle, pictured below left, is one of the highest and most remote pubs in England, standing on the moors at 1,690ft (507m). Undecorated and austere, the tiny Jenkin Chapel, below right, was built in 1733 from local gritstone and named after a local sheepfarming family. The tower is a later addition from 1754. Although originally dedicated to St John the Baptist, the chapel was not consecrated until 1794 when it was re-dedicated to St John the Evangelist.

YOULGRAVE

On the banks of the river Bradford, shortly before it meets the river Lathkill, Youlgrave (or Youlgreave, as it is sometimes spelt), is an ancient village three miles south of Bakewell

Youlgrave, known locally for unknown reasons as 'Pommie', is the largest of three villages – Bradford, Alport and Middleton – which lie close to one another amidst classic limestone countryside. The village is famous for its collection of curious buildings, including the large circular water tank, known as The Fountain, pictured left. It was once used as a storage tank for water pumped from the nearby river Bradford to supply the village.

The 13th century All Saints Church is considered second only in importance to the church of St John the Baptist at Tideswell. Its perpendicular tower can be seen from all over the village. Follow the river Bradford in the direction of Alport and the road from Youlgrave crosses the river Lathkill, pictured right. Narrow Lathkill Dale, with its steep-sided gorge, is one of the most beautiful in the Peaks.